Red-eared guenon

Spider monkey

The monkeys and apes brought together in this book come from many different countries all over the world.

Hanuman monkey

Japanese macaque

Spider monkeys

Now when the sun comes up
it's hungry monkey time.
Time to look for fruit and leaves.
Time for breakfast on a branch.

I like monkeys because...
I like the way they huddle.
I like the way they cuddle.

These are Spectacled langurs.
They have bright-orange babies.

I like the way they clean each other's fur.

Hanuman monkeys like these are sacred in India.

I like monkeys because...
I like the funny way they play.
Young ones tease and trick, then
scamper off as fast as they can go.

I like monkeys because...
I like the way they jump
from branch to branch,
from tree to tree.

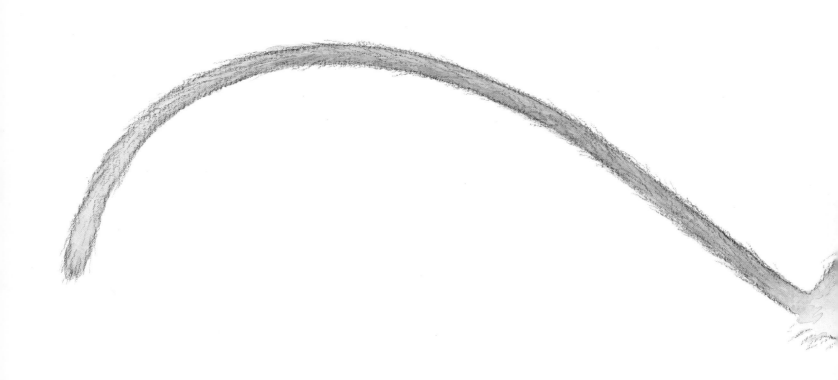

What a mighty leap!

Some
monkeys'
tails
are
longer
than
their
bodies.

Black-and-white colobus

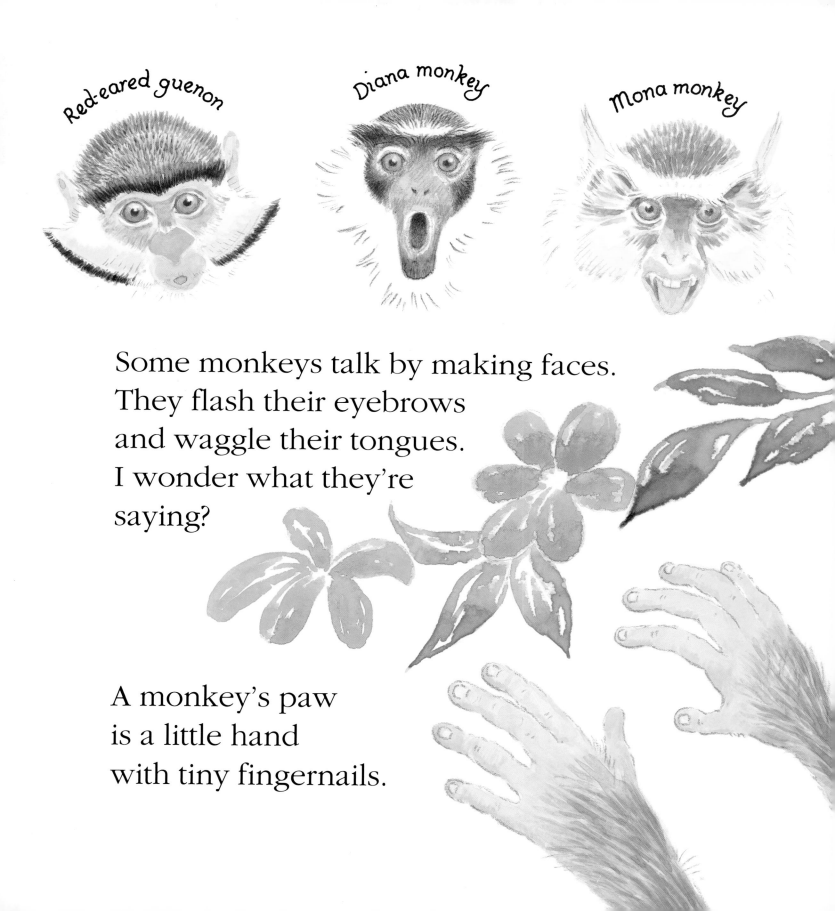

Red-eared guenon

Diana monkey

Mona monkey

Some monkeys talk by making faces.
They flash their eyebrows
and waggle their tongues.
I wonder what they're
saying?

A monkey's paw
is a little hand
with tiny fingernails.

I like baby monkeys because...
they scream and
rush about and
leap and scold
and shriek and
wave their arms
and pull and tug

and cause
all sorts
of bother.

Mother carries baby
tucked up underneath
or riding piggyback.
Baby knows to
hang on tight.

Rhesus monkeys are tough and adaptable.
They've even been sent into space.

A Black-and-white colobus is often hard to spot in a tree.
Its fur looks like hanging moss.

This monkey is beautiful
and black and white
and hairy.

Uakari

This monkey
has a bald
head.

These monkeys
have long
noses.

male Proboscis monkey

female Proboscis monkey

Now when the sun is high
it's lazy monkey time.
Time to have some lunch.
Time to stretch and yawn.
Time to groom and chatter.

These are tiny Squirrel monkeys.

These are big Baboons.

*Japanese macaques like to bathe in warm water.
They wash their potatoes in it, too.*

These monkeys keep nice and
warm in their volcanic pool.
Can you think of a better way
to spend a snowy afternoon?

"Orang-utan" means "man of the forest" in Malay.

These young apes think
the rain is just a pain.

Orang-utans don't like water.

This Gorilla is the biggest ape of all.

Gorillas are especially gentle.

Now when the sun is setting
it's time to settle down.
Time to make a nest of leaves.
Time to cuddle up and snooze.

These apes are Chimpanzees.

They always sleep in the treetops.

Squirrel monkey

Monkeys

Baboon

Black-and-white colobus

Diana monkey

Hanuman monkey

Japanese macaque

Mona monkey

Proboscis monkey

Red-eared guenon

Rhesus monkey

Spectacled langur

Spider monkey

Squirrel monkey

Uakari

Apes

Chimpanzee

Gorilla

Orang-utan

Now look back through the book and see if you can find all these apes and monkeys.

Baboon

Chimpanzee